When a child asks to be baptised

When a child asks to be baptised

Daphne Kirk

First published in 1999 by
KEVIN MAYHEW LTD
Buxhall
Stowmarket
Suffolk IP14 3DJ

0 1 2 3 4 5 6 7 8 9

ISBN 1 84003 323 1
Catalogue No 1500248

Cover designed by Jaquetta Sergeant
Edited by Helen Elliot
Typesetting by Louise Selfe
Printed and bound in Great Britain

Contents

Introduction

When a child asks to be baptised many questions often surface – questions such as

- Are they ready to be baptised?
- How can we help them understand?
- What part do the parents play, and should we involve them?
- How can the cell play a part?

This book seeks to answer these and other questions. While biblical principles and their application are unchanging, some of the practical ideas may seem very directive. They have been tried, tested and found to be very effective, so are presented here in order that each Cell Church can make them their own, perhaps adapting or changing elements to suit the local practice of baptism. Use them as a springboard for your own situation!

It is difficult to write solely about children in the context of baptism, for the majority of the principles and practice apply equally to adults, and recognition of this fact will liberate many churches to receive little ones into the Kingdom on the same terms as adults. It is interesting that *we* are commanded to be like *them!*

In fact, much of what is contained in this book also applies to adults; this is not about something new for children, but about ensuring that they have the same opportunities as adults, and that parents retain their parental responsibilities and involvement. One dynamic that must make a difference when considering baptising children is that parents are ultimately responsible for their children and need to be involved in the decisions surrounding this important event in the life of their child.

This book assumes that, from the moment the child asks to be baptised, the cell leader takes the 'pastoral role' with the child.

This book presupposes that the Church believes:

- Jesus is the Son of God, for after Jesus' baptism the Spirit 'descended on Him like a dove and a voice came from heaven: "You are my Son, whom I love: with you I am well pleased."' (Mark 1:10-11)

- His death was part of God's plan of salvation; as Peter said on the day of Pentecost, in Acts 2:23: 'This man was handed over to you by God's set purpose and foreknowledge, and you, with the help of wicked men, put Him to death by nailing Him to the cross.'

- Jesus rose from the dead having conquered death, and is alive today. Acts 2:24 says: 'But God raised Him from the dead, freeing Him from the agony of death, because it was impossible for death to keep its hold on Him.'

- Jesus is seated at the right hand of God and is coming again as described in Acts 1:11: 'This same Jesus . . . will come back in the same way you have seen Him go into heaven.'

- Everyone (adults, young people and children) has sinned. In Romans 3:23 it clearly states that 'all have sinned and fall short of the glory of God'.

- Everyone (adults, young people and children) needs to repent, be baptised and be forgiven as is clearly stated in Acts 2:38: 'Repent and be baptised, every one of you, in the name of Jesus Christ for the forgiveness of your sins.'

- Everyone (adults, young people and children) needs to receive the gift of the Holy Spirit, for Acts 2:38 continues, 'and you will receive the gift of the Holy Spirit. The promise is for you and your children.'

- Everyone (adults, young people and children) must call on Jesus for salvation. Acts 2:21 promises that 'everyone who calls on the name of the Lord will be saved'.

- Everyone (adults, young people and children) must be baptised as a sign that the past is buried and that new life has begun. Acts 2:38 has already been quoted: 'Repent and be baptised, every one of you.'

- Baptism follows a personal commitment to Jesus. Mark 16:16 clearly states that 'whoever believes and is baptised will be saved'.

- Baptism is 'in the name of the Father and of the Son and of the Holy Spirit', as found in Matthew 28:19 where Jesus commissions His disciples to 'go and make disciples of all nations, baptising them in the name of the Father and of the Son and of the Holy Spirit'.

- Baptism is a response taken in faith and obedience to the command that we have already read in Matthew 28:19.

- Baptism is a confession before men, for Jesus said, in Matthew 10:32-33, 'Whoever acknowledges me before men I will also acknowledge before my Father in heaven, but whoever disowns me before men, I will disown before my Father in heaven'.

- Baptism is identification with Jesus. Romans 6:3-14 clearly sets out the process by which baptism is identifying with the death and resurrection of the Lord Jesus Christ.

- Baptism is *in* (signifying death) . . . *under* (signifying burial) . . . and *out* (signifying resurrection) of the water, fulfilling the parallel with Jesus' death and resurrection which we have already seen in Romans 6:3-14. This is also demonstrated in Acts 8:38-39 when 'Philip and the eunuch went down into the water and Philip baptised him . . . they came up out of the water . . .'

- Talking to a child about baptism is not really very different from talking to an adult. The biblical principles for baptising are not affected by race, gender, denomination or age.

How much should the child understand?

Each child can understand enough, depending on where they are spiritually and intellectually (but that is the same with adults) and it should always be remembered that the criteria for baptism are that the child (or adult) has been born again and has repented of their sin.

Every person, adult or child, will understand more as they grow in Jesus. In Scripture we see time and again that baptism should follow immediately after conversion. When we are in situations where baptism is delayed for practical, traditional or religious reasons, it is good that we use the time to increase the child's (or adult's) understanding, always remembering that understanding alone is not the deciding factor for baptism.

When talking with the child use language you know they will understand, and sit comfortably at their level, then take it step by step, always encouraging and always seeing any obstacle in their life as a miracle for God to overcome!

> **Remember that baptism is not about what the child (or adult) understands . . . but about what they have done!**
>
> **Have they repented and been born again of the Spirit of God?**

If you should have any questions about the 'right' of children to be baptised, the answer is probably the same as with adults! For example:

'I've known children turn away from God after baptism.'
I've known adults do that, too!

'Children don't all understand.'
Neither do all adults.

'We can't really be sure about some of their conversions.'
We can't really be sure about all adults.

'They may regret it when they are older.'
Some adults do, too!

**If you believe that baptism is a command
and that it is a powerful moment that
releases the blessing of God . . .**

**can we deny our children the opportunity
to obey and receive that blessing?**

Chapter 1
_____Talking with the Child _____

When a child asks to be baptised, the first thing to establish is whether they have asked their parents. Always check with the parents yourself before you explore the issue any further with the child. If the parents agree . . .

Talk to the child about why they have asked to be baptised

Remember that they may express the reason in a very childish way. Never be put off by an unspiritual answer. Their first reply does not necessarily indicate their spiritual standing. For example, if they should say that it is just, 'Because I want to be,' or 'Because I want to go into the water,' we need to remember that most children ask before they have had the opportunity of understanding about baptism. However, this gives the opening to talk further with them, not to dismiss their request.

Do you witness that they are born again?

Their life within the community or cell will speak louder than their words! Can you give adequate expression to the life of God in you, even with the vocabulary that you have acquired during your adult years?

Have they a simple testimony?

Remember that the word _testimony_ is very ambiguous, so simple questions may help them to express themselves. The following are not designed to be delivered like an exam, but as openers for conversations that will lead to the child having a greater under-standing about their life with Jesus, and being better able to express what that means to them.

- Do you love Jesus?
- Do you think that Jesus loves you?
- What has He done to show you that He loves you very much?
- Why do you think that Jesus died on the cross?

Then we can help them to understand more about repentance as it touches their lives by starting with questions such as:

- Why did Jesus have to die?
- Does it matter to Jesus if we are naughty?
- How do you feel when you are naughty?
- What do you do when you know you have been naughty? (Say sorry to Jesus and the person wronged, then decide not to do it again.)

If they are not born again, they may want to take that step with you

Don't miss this opportunity to share the love of Jesus with them! Too often, when children (or adults) ask for baptism, it is seen as a 'pass or fail' question, instead of a wonderful opportunity to spend time together and see where they are in their relationship with Jesus.

If you are in agreement with their being baptised . . .

Talk to your coordinator, and check they are in agreement and then find out when the next date for a baptism will be.

Always arrange to meet the child with the parents present

It is essential that the parent hears the explanation for baptism, so they can then talk with the child about it in the same way and avoid confusion. This involves the parents every step of the way and increases the sense of security for the child. It builds unity around the child as the child experiences their parents and the cell working together on their behalf.

If the parents are not Christians it shows that you honour and respect them, maintaining parental responsibility. It also gives them another opportunity to hear the Gospel and perhaps have some of their own questions answered.

Every child should have the opportunity of going through the baptism explanation

Do not teach them but allow them to tell you as much as they are able, and you fill in the gaps. This will give you the opportunity of seeing what they already understand.

* You will discover what they are thinking
  – not what you believed they were thinking!
* You will discover what they know
  – not what you thought they knew!

The result will be that you will be able to lead them gently on from that place.

This time is about your relationship with the child and the family

It is really important to appreciate this, so do not underestimate the value of the time you spend with them.

Summary

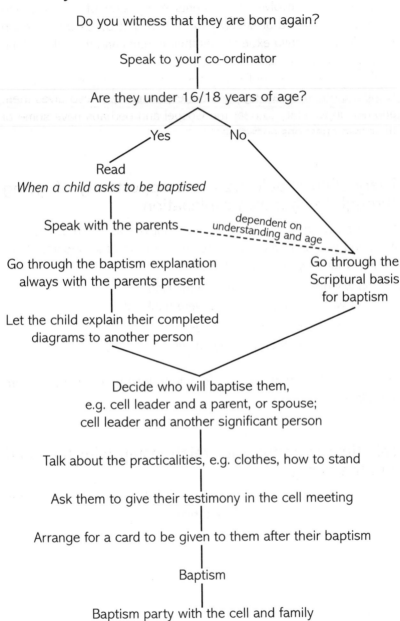

Do you witness that they are born again?

Speak to your co-ordinator

Are they under 16/18 years of age?

Yes   No

Read
When a child asks to be baptised

Speak with the parents — dependent on understanding and age

Go through the baptism explanation
always with the parents present

Go through the
Scriptural basis
for baptism

Let the child explain their completed
diagrams to another person

Decide who will baptise them,
e.g. cell leader and a parent, or spouse;
cell leader and another significant person

Talk about the practicalities, e.g. clothes, how to stand

Ask them to give their testimony in the cell meeting

Arrange for a card to be given to them after their baptism

Baptism

Baptism party with the cell and family

Chapter 2
Exploring the Meaning of Baptism

The following are exploratory questions or statements to help open a meaningful conversation with a child who has asked to be baptised. They are not intended to be delivered as a list, but rather as pointers to give a sense of direction to your conversation. Above all, they are not pass or fail questions.

We want everyone to be born again of the Spirit of God and baptised, so use these suggestions as opportunities to explain where necessary, for the child to respond, and for you to minister to the child. Remember to include the parent in your sharing together, but be careful always to keep the child as the focus.

Share together about the special occasions that the cell celebrates. The child will probably think of many – take an interest in them all! Eventually mention baptism. Find out if the child has ever seen a baptism. If they have, ask them to tell you all about it.

Read Mark 1:9-11 together. Use the child's Bible to read from as that is the one that they will be used to. If at all possible, ask them to read it to you first, then you read it to them. Then either . . .

- draw a picture together of what happened in the reading

or

- ask the child to pretend that you could not understand what was read and ask them to tell you what it was all about.

Draw the following diagrams very slowly, letting the child explain as much as they can to you as you ask simple questions. The 'answers' (in brackets) are the place you eventually want to get to. The child may say many other things first; do not dismiss them but continue to share until you reach the required point to complete the drawing.

Diagram 1
Where do we have our baptisms? (Draw the pool.)

What are we baptised in? (Add the water.)

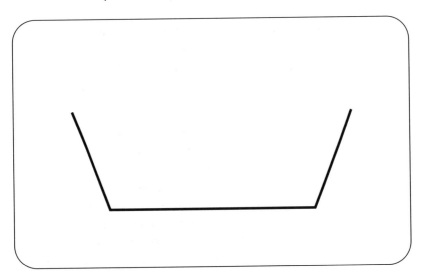

What happens to us when we are in the water? (We go into the water, under it, then come up out of it again – draw the arrows.)

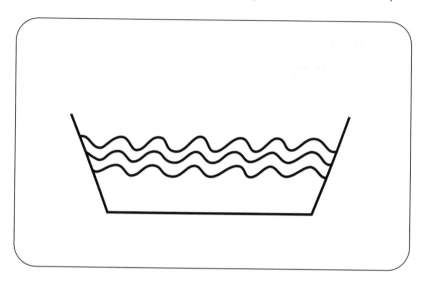

Diagram 2

How did Jesus die? (Draw the cross and spend some time talking together about why He died.)

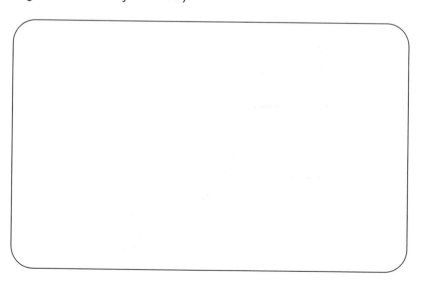

What happened to His body after He had died? (It went down into the tomb. Draw the tomb and the line going down.)

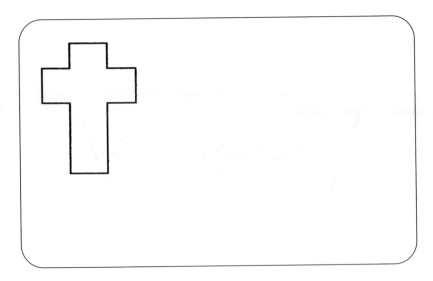

Then what happened? (He came alive again. Finish the drawing.)

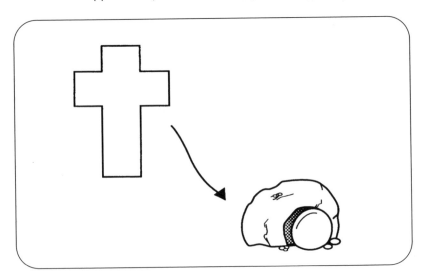

Romans 6:3-11 (The *Youth Bible* has been used here.) This is a long passage. You will have to use your discretion about how much, if any of it, you actually read. Primarily it is for you as background for the third diagram. Verse 3 can be talked about by all ages. Children accept these things far more easily than adults, which is why Jesus told us to be like them!

'. . . all of us became part of Christ when we were baptised' Romans 6:3

Talk about the wonder of how this can be. Give the child time to express thoughts and feelings about this before you use the following diagram to explain the passage from Romans 6.

Diagram 3
'We shared His death in our baptism' (verse 3).
Draw the cross.

'We were buried with Christ and shared His death' (verse 4).
Draw the tomb.

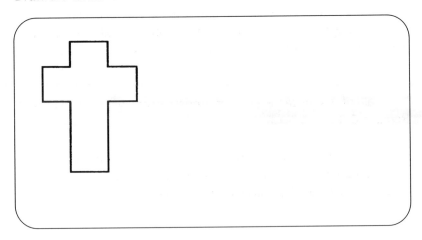

Ask the child if they have any idea how this could be. Listen to their ideas, then say that the best thing to do in order to find out is to look a bit further and see if the Bible tells us how.

'So, just as Christ was raised from the dead by the wonderful power of the Father, we also can live a new life' (verse 4).
Draw the 'resurrection' symbol.

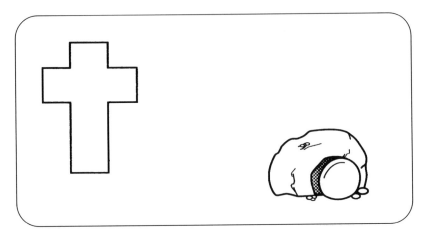

Express pleasure that we don't only share the death and burial but the resurrection as well!

'We know that our old life died with Christ on the cross . . .' (verse 6).

Share with the child what our old lives looked like. What were we like before we knew Jesus? Identify sins by name, for example, calling people names, being disobedient. Together, write some of these things on the cross, being sure to put some of your past sins on, as well as the child's!

' . . . so that our sinful selves would have no power over us' (verse 6). Ask the child if dead people can do anything to or for us. (Don't get drawn into discussing ghosts!) Then ask, if our sin is dead, can it have power over us? Can it make us do things?

'We know that our old life died with Christ on the cross, so our sinful selves would have no power over us' (verse 6).

Talk together about the fact that baptism shows that our old self has been defeated on the cross by Jesus when He died. It has been buried. Draw the pool and the water showing that, just as Jesus went to be buried in the tomb, so our old life is buried under the water.

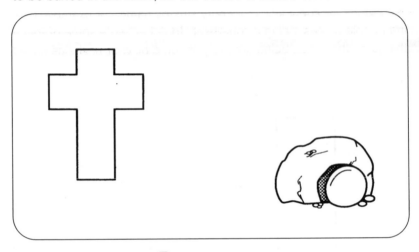

'[Jesus] has a new life, and His new life is with God' (verse 10) and we have a new life. Draw the 'resurrection' symbol.

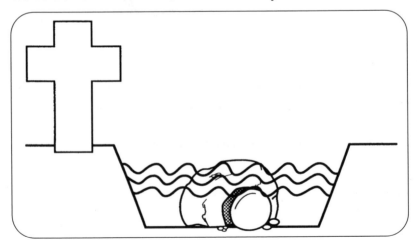

Explain that we have a new life too. Ask the child what our new life is like. Don't just be spiritual, it can sound so boring – include things like fun and good friends as well as receiving and giving love and suchlike.

Finally, add the arrows as you say that we go down into the water to show that our old life has been dead and buried, and that we come out again to show the new life that we have in Jesus; so the final drawing should look like this:

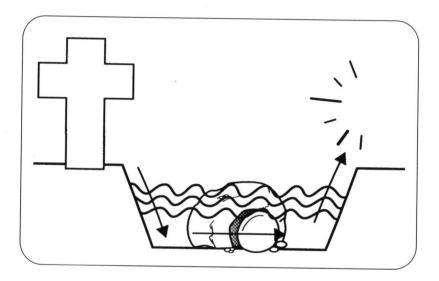

Give the child the opportunity to ask questions about what you have just done, though if you have explained slowly they should have raised most of these as you went along.

The child might like to explain the drawings to you, pretending that you don't know what it is all about. (This will give you a clear idea of what they have understood.)

Give the child a copy of pages 28 to 31 and ask them to fill them in. Arrange to receive them at your next cell meeting. Finish by praying with the child (and parents), letting the child pray, too.

Remember, at the next cell meeting, to take great interest in the sheets that the child has completed. Perhaps you might find a co-operative person and let the child show them the completed sheets and explain what they are about. (Another chance to go over it!)

Baptism

There are some very special times you will share with your cell group.

He b _ _ _ _ _ _ _ Him.

Baptism is when someone who is following Jesus goes into the water, right under it and then comes up again.

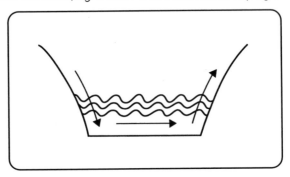

Jesus died on the cross, was buried in the grave and came alive again.

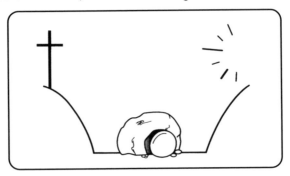

So we show that our old life is dead and buried and that we have a new life in the Kingdom of God.

Being baptised is really important.
It is something Jesus did and something He told us to do.

Now read Romans 6:4

We were therefore _ _ _ _ _ _ with

Him through baptism into _ _ _ _ _

in order that, just as _ _ _ _ _ _ was

raised from the dead through the

glory of the _ _ _ _ _ _ , we too may

live a _ _ _ _ _ _ _ .

Do you understand these verses? . . . If you said 'No', your special friend will help you.

29

**Can you draw the special pictures
that tell us all about being baptised?**

Baptism is when someone who is following
Jesus goes into the water, right under it and then comes up again.

Jesus died on the cross, was buried in the grave and came alive again.

So we show that our old life is dead and buried and we have a new life in the Kingdom of God.

Being baptised is really important.
It is something Jesus did and something He told us to do.

Q Where in the Bible is this explained to us?

Have you ever seen anyone baptised? Yes / No

If you have, could you tell me about it, or draw a picture?

Chapter 3
_____ Involving the Parents _____

When a child asks to be baptised, how can the cell leader involve parents, recognising their unique place in the life of the child? If the parents are not Christians, how can the child's request be seen as an opportunity rather than a problem? This chapter addresses some of these issues.

Parents need to remain fully involved

Ultimately the decision about the child's baptism is their responsibility. Too often in the body of Christ that responsibility has not been recognised or honoured, which has resulted in causing, rather than resolving, conflict between child and parent.

If the parent is the pastor, or another leader in the Church

It makes no difference; treat them as parents, for that is what is important during this time. It is important for the child, and often a relief for the parents to enjoy the freedom of being treated as parents rather than pastors or leaders who happen to be parents! Too often the roles of church leader and parent are merged, leading to confusion. Similarly, if the parent is also the cell leader, ask the cell leader in training to assume the pastoral role and release the cell leader to be mum or dad.

If the parents are not Christians

They are still the parents! Too often non-Christian parents are disregarded and can feel ostracised by the church, or cell, of which their child is a part. This is a wonderful opportunity to honour them and develop friendship. Many parents will be impressed that you value them, their feelings, and their place in the child's life. Within the context of relationship you have an opportunity to talk with (not at) them about why you baptise people, and why it is important to their child.

If the parents disagree

Should the parents not agree to their child being baptised, there are many ways to use this opportunity as a part of the process of winning them to Jesus. (Remember that they need Jesus and the child needs them to know Jesus!) This is not the time for winning an argument about baptism.

Pray for them, spend time with them, listen to them and give them the space and opportunity to express their concerns and opinions. Allow the Holy Spirit to convict – it is not your task.

The next step you take will depend on how receptive they are to the Gospel, and how many of the cell members are their friends. It may be important to introduce them to the cell members informally by inviting them to your home or to a social event you are holding. Maybe there are needs that the cell could meet; for example, do they need a baby-sitter?

On the other hand, if they were willing, they could be invited to a forthcoming baptismal service, even if their own child is not being baptised. It is very possible that they have never seen what happens at a baptism and would like to see exactly what their child is considering.

If the parents agree

Go through the same process of preparing the child with them present, of course not forgetting to invite them to the baptism, and to someone's home afterwards for something to eat! Make sure a seat is reserved for them (they may find the front row rather threatening, so a few rows back might be a good idea) and ensure a cell member waits for them (or collects them), hosting and introducing them to other cell members.

Finally – a revolutionary thought – have you considered that one of them might like to baptise the child with the cell leader? It is on the basis of the child's faith, not theirs, that the baptism is taking place; could it be rather like a wedding, 'giving the child to Jesus'? This is just a thought worth considering, thinking about, to agree with or disagree with.

If the parents are Christians and active members of the cell

They still need the opportunity to be involved, and to have their views honoured. Whatever your personal relationship with them, throughout this process they are primarily the child's parents.

If the parents are Christians but do not want their child baptised

Listen carefully, pray and show that you will honour them. The following may prove helpful in sharing with children whose parents have said, for whatever reason, that they do not agree with them being baptised.

My own daughter, Daniella, wanted to be baptised, but our pastors at that time did not agree with children being baptised.

Now Daniella knew that her older sisters had been baptised as children, and she loved Jesus with all her little heart. When she tearfully looked to me for an answer, I said to her: 'Daniella, there is something more important than being right. I want you to use this time to learn something really special, something that many adults never learn – I want you to wait with a happy and willing heart. I want you to trust Jesus with this.'

And for many years she did, though at times it was a struggle, and I had to reaffirm what I had already told her.

However, God turned the hearts of the pastors, and the day came when she was baptised. On the morning of her baptism I said to her, with such joy in my heart: 'Daniella, I am so proud of you. You kept your heart sweet, you did not get resentful. I am even pleased that God gave you this opportunity.'

It was a precious moment, one that I shall cherish for the rest of my life, and one I hope she will remember when she needs to know that sometimes 'there is something more important than being right'!

I hope this illustration may help, if you wish to share it with children whose parents, whether Christians or not, say 'No' to their child being baptised at that time. It may be that you need to remember it yourself, should you ever be tempted to feel resentful about a parent's response, or about other similar situations in your own life!

Chapter 4

———— Involving the Cell ————

Listed below are some questions that will help you to consider how much and in what ways you wish to involve the cell when baptisms take place. These suggestions will obviously apply to adults, young people and children for there should be no distinction between the way that people are baptised. There is one baptism, one Lord and one Church!

- How will you involve or give ownership to the cell?
- How will you acknowledge the place that the cell leader plays in the child's (or adult's) life?
- How will this very special time be celebrated within the cell?

. . . and here are some ideas.

- Just before the event, ask the child (or adult) to tell the cell that they are going to be baptised and to share with them why this is important to them. They could also be asked to share about the time when they knew that they had given their lives over to Jesus. It is reasonable to expect that everyone will be able to share within their cell, but very inhibiting for some to share with the whole Church. I have known adults refuse baptism because they felt unable to address the whole Church. Children are no different; some might find the entire congregation very inhibiting. Sharing with people they know, who love and accept them, is completely different.

- The cell could pray for them, and, if there are words of prophecy for them, ask someone to write them down on a card, to be signed by the whole group and the senior pastor and given to them at their baptism.

- It might be an idea for the whole cell to move forward around the baptismal pool at the moment of baptism, giving them the place of honour, front row involvement!

- A key question is, who will baptise the child? Asking the cell leader to baptise the child with one of the parents is very meaningful for all concerned. We have found that both the leader and the parent consider this a great honour and a very moving experience. It also makes it a very secure moment for the child.

- Taking a photograph of all the members of the cell, with the child (or adult) central and perhaps giving the child (or adult) a card, signed by all the members of the cell, provides a very personal reminder of their day.

These ideas are not intended to add to the baptism – nothing can do that – but they do highlight its importance, and maintain the values of being a Cell Church.

Chapter 5

Testimonies

The following are testimonies given at various times by members of intergenerational cells, after their own baptisms, or those of their children.

'To be baptised feels like all the sin has been washed off and when you go under it feels like you have died and when you come back up it feels like you live a new life.' David, aged 7.

'Getting baptised made me feel more close to God and bolder to do God's work. I'm pleased that I chose to get baptised.' James, aged 9.

'Being baptised made me realise how great God is. It also made me feel like I was becoming grown up. I am glad I got baptised. James, aged 9.

'When my children were baptised it was a very special day to witness them taking a step of faith on their own. I've watched them continuing to grow in the Lord in our family and in our cell. To express my feelings that day is difficult to put into words but I am so blessed with my family.' Doreen (parent).

'The concept of an Intergenerational Church is that we are all ministers and it was that which enabled us to fulfil a long-standing dream and prayer, that of baptising our four children, as husband and wife, mum and dad. It was such an honour and a pleasure and created closer bonds between us and our children and God. The whole baptism was very special and very alive; a special and unforgettable time which was followed by a wonderful cell celebration and party at home.' Chris and Francesca (parents).

'We all know that the call of God is as real and true to our children as it is to any adults. As our two boys James and David (aged 7 and 9) got older, they expressed a wish to be baptised. As with many churches, it was not the practice to baptise children under the age of about 13. However, when we considered that we asked our children to adhere to the teachings of Christ concerning their morals, actions and future life, it appeared hypocritical to deny them obedience to this very important command.

Some would say that they were too young to understand what they were doing. My reply would be that, if that were the case, then they were too young to understand what it meant to be saved, when in fact they could read the commands of our Lord as easily as the next person.

As a parent I feel that my children made a decision to follow their Saviour based on the knowledge and experience they had, which is no more or less than any of us can do. What's more, I feel I have fulfilled my duty as a parent in allowing them to seek after the one true God for themselves.' Mark and Sandra (parents).

Intergenerational
_____ Cell Church Seminars _____

These seminars are for you if you can identify with any of the following:

- Have you wondered how to integrate your children and young people totally into the body of Christ?
- Are you lacking the resources and training and therefore unsure of the way forward?
- Do you wonder how your church can have one vision and move together, adults, young people and children?
- Do you want your whole church to grow, learn and experience kingdom life in the way God intended . . . together?
- Are you cell church and wanting to integrate the children?

Important points with regard to seminars:

(a)   The seminars are visionary with a strong biblical foundation as well as very practical, with their emphasis being on the outworking of the vision in the local church.

(b)   It is essential for the senior leadership to attend the seminar in order to carry the vision to their own congregation. However, the format is kept simple so that anyone can participate and lead intergenerational groups.

(c)   Seminars vary between one and three days, depending on the number of workshops held. Obviously the longer the seminar, the more practical experience and personal application can be incorporated. Churches usually have seminars for Friday evening and all day Saturday.

(d)   Seminars include discussion of, and where possible some experience of, the intergenerational celebration and corporate prayer life of the church. Leaders of worship, celebration and prayer meetings are strongly encouraged to attend.

(e)   A manual will be used so that leaders can replicate the seminar with their own church. However, the more people from your church who attend the seminar, the clearer will be the vision and the greater the anointing taken back.

If you are considering being an intergenerational church or having intergenerational cells and would like to host or attend one of Daphne Kirk's seminars contact her at:

The Lighthouse Centre
13 Lynn Road
Ely
Cambs
CB7 4EG

Telephone: 01353 662228
Fax: 01353 662179
E-mail: ecf@lhouse.win-uk.net

Materials Available to Facilitate ___ the Intergenerational Cell ___

There are currently two books of meeting outlines:

Book 1
* Relationships (based on the Book of Ruth)
* Extracts from 1 Timothy

Book 2
* Who will be a servant?
* The Lord's Supper
* Prayer

Each pack consists of meeting outlines, each section being a series for four weeks. These give detailed instructions on every section of the meeting, including the icebreaker and the offering.

Hand in Hand: sponsoring a child using 'Living with Jesus – an equipping track for children'.

Living with Jesus – an equipping track for children. Eight books which take child and adult together through the fundamentals of the Christian faith.

Available from:

The Lighthouse Centre, 13 Lynn Road, Ely, Cambs CB7 4EG

Telephone: 01353 662228
Fax: 01353 662179
E-mail: ecf@lhouse.win-uk.net

Bibliography and
____ Recommended Reading ____

Heirs together, Daphne Kirk, published by Kevin Mayhew.

Hand in hand: sponsoring a child using 'Living with Jesus – an equipping track for children', Daphne Kirk, published by Kevin Mayhew.

The second reformation, William A. Beckham, published by TOUCH Publications, PO Box 19888, Houston TX77224.

Where do we go from here? Ralph W. Neighbour, published by TOUCH Publications.

The shepherd's guidebook, Ralph W. Neighbour, published by TOUCH Publications.

Sowing, reaping, keeping, Laurence Singlehurst, published by Crossway Books, an imprint of IVP, Norton Street, Nottingham NG7 3HR.

Cell iT, by Laurence Singlehurst, *An equipping track for adults, 'Passion' for youth,* and *CellChurch Magazine* are all available from the Lighthouse Centre, 13 Lynn Road, Ely, Cambridgeshire CB7 4EG.